The Best of

COW TIPPING PRESS

VOLUME 2

Introduction
by Henry Hietala

My aunt has a developmental disability. Because of her, I
have always had an interest in neurodiversity, which led
to me teaching a workshop for Cow Tipping Press. My
experience was incredible. While I hope my students
learned more than I did, like most teachers, I suspect that
was not the case. The students challenged me in discussion
and in print, forcing me to rethink all of my preconceived
notions of disability. Now, every time I visit my aunt in
California, I feel a tinge of regret. Yes, I am grateful for the
work of her group home staff, but part of me wishes she
had access to a program like Cow Tipping. She would
definitely benefit from it.

But this anthology isn't about me. It's a showcase for the
varied, vital work of 17 Cow Tipping authors. Their stories
run the full gauntlet of human emotion. "Pepper Spray"
is a harrowing look at personal danger in a public space.
The swimming pool slapstick of "Hot to Handle" had me
laughing so hard I got a couple dirty looks in the subway.
Shelagh Winkel's "Spidercat" is a fable about unlikely

combinations, and Danny Roherty's "Birdy" enters the realm of contemporary myth.

The writers are genre-agnostic in the best possible way, mixing memoir and reportage, poetry and prose. They speak their truth, no matter how strange or discomfiting it may be. As Mary Ayetey writes, "I don't want your lies." If you're looking for comfortable, safe sentences, then read no further. But if you prefer writing that puzzles, challenges, and ultimately changes you, then read on. This anthology is for you.

Tourature Chamber
by Eric Ferguson

I called 911
My dad was so mad
I got sent to my room
My mom didn't want anything to do with me
I learned to never call 911 again
I called 911

Ghazal
by Mike Ruland

Oh my atlanta Someone ate
the plate of cake no one is Looking cake

my brother and me like to eat
cake

I went to the store and brought
some food for the holiday to Celebrate John F. Kennedy
cake

cake

cake

cake

Lipstick and Turnbuckles
by Justin Beebe

Wrestling has been going on since the 1800s. It started in carnivals, circuses and fairs. They've had people like Mildred Burke, Betty Boucher, June Byers, and many more. They've even had mixed matches where the guys would go up against the girls in tag teams and singles. They'd even compete in boxing matches. The promoter would offer $100 to any man who could beat them in the ring and every man lost except one because one of them knocked out Mildred—the wrestlers in the match—and that's how the guy won.

I've always wanted to be in the ring with a girl myself. I want to be like Andy Kaufman—they called him the Intergender Wrestling Champion. He challenged women in the ring and he beat them every time. If a woman beat him they would marry him and he continued until his retirement.

They've also had celebrities get in the ring like Don Imus, Bill Cosby and others. And one wrestler I remember is

Chyna because she was a powerhouse. She wrestled men in the ring and also watched them.

"WOW women are wrestling on TV." They were promoted on wrestling channel David McClean. That was on channel six. That's how I got into women's wrestling.

It was better than men's wrestling and it was more entertaining to men because I wanted to be a bad guy wrestler, to be with the girls.

"Women should be in the kitchen, cooking, cleaning, producing the babies." Andy Kaufman. Men loved him, women hated him. Women's wrestling is a popular sport— it's been around for a long time. I'm really happy to be a fan of women's wrestling.

Trace Memory
by Kong Moua

I wake up on the boat it is morning I go to the deck. The wind is cool the water is cold I feel the water as I put my hand in the cool water. I am nervous uneasy the waves are very shaky and the birds are catching fish. My memory of my mom in my head.

Balloon
by Stephanie Hart

You lost a balloon
Couldn't find it
In the Whisper.

A Closet
by Max Cookas

Start with *kazzam!* A bench or a couch and with a window, glass. His coat, with his shirt kind of like it looks freezing. Don't get with a sunburn, his stomach, yes.

Start with a remote, will hit a storm, TV or maybe the basement, yes, mancave.

Otherwise a bed, a pillow with a storm. Or microwave with a storm or gusher, toilet, sink and then that's it.

Pepper Spray
by Mary Ayetey

It was Christmas last year. I thought I wanted cookbooks for Christmas, but instead I got pepperspray. It just looks mysterious and so strange. I've got to use it carefully, leave it at home and not let anyone know about it. It's no toy it's no prank it's a test it's self defense my stepdad says "emergencies only" he said emergencies only.

I was walking in the woods out at night. There was a strange guy stalking me and I turned around and pepperspray them. Then I ran off and call for help looking shocked. A future stepmother came up asks her "are you okay what happened?" I was calm saying "this guy tries to follow me" it was made out of red fire and it burns like red fire the guy burns like redfire.

Best Friends Forever
by Caleb Gutz

Dear Sam Baumann,

I have happy Tears comes to mine when you are Gifted by God that's why you are the best thing of my whole Life and to call you my buddy I am every proud of you with all you do because you bring a Lot Joy and Loving Man as you are That's why you Give me happy Tears.

She Doesn't Want to Be in a Wheelchair Anymore
by Kelly McNamera

She was an ugly lady. She was short and super skinny. She had short, greasy red hair. As red as a fire truck. She never showered so the smell of garbage reeked off her. She was a crabby lady. Always yelling and backtalking. She spent most of her time at work. She was a receptionist. She was awful at this job and got fired. She was a human garbage can. She acts like a hooker and was all by herself. She knew that in order to be happy she needed friends. She lives in Texas. She is in a wheelchair and this is why she is so angry.

Merry Christmas
by Caleb Gutz

I saw a Picktures it Feels Like Christmas and we can't see What is Going on but it's Fun to pray out there and I can't how to see Fog it Feels like Art and it's so detailed with joy and brings you a lot of laughter and it brings you out into the community. Peace on earth and good will. Tiding. Temperature. The sun comes out and melts the fog.

Ghazal
by Maddie Wild Crea

My youngest brother Peter Peter
Peter very kind and helpful Peter

Peter always studies hard. He
and I try to see each other on weekends.

Peter is a natrual athleete
He is a junior in High School Peter.

He wants to do something
in either Math or science sometime.

Peter has a smile that looks as
if he was thinking only of you.

Birdy
by Danny Roherty

I was out fishing and I caught a couple fish, then I said to myself one more cast. I then cast the line and within seconds I got a tug on it. I started to wheel in and on the end of the line is a bird. I was like, a bird who thinks he is a fish. I then take a picture of me and the bird on the line then take the hook out of its beak. I place it on the boat and it doesn't fly away. It just sits there looking at me.

I take it to my car and drive away back home. I then get a tank from my basement and fill it with water. I place the bird inside it. It swims around and occasionally comes up for air. Then goes back down into the water and swims. I have never seen a bird who loved to swim as much as he did. It was a very unusual sight to see.

Then I go to record and post a video of the Bird-Fish. It gets over a million views on YouTube and over 200,000 likes and shares. I am now famous with a bird-fish. Who

would have thought a bird would think it's a fish and do
what that bird does? Not me in a million years.

About My Heart
by Mike Ruland

I was a kid I had heart surgery they open my heart they replace it put it back in me I have a scar my mom is shocked to see mom was happy to see it then they stitch it up my scar I ate the peanut and got stuck in my throat and my parents cpr me mom and dad called the Doctor they took me in check me out and it's happy ending.

on "About My Heart"
by Laura Berglund

In "about my heart," Mike Ruland describes the actions and
emotions of others while moving between the past and
present tenses. He captures the tumult of both heart
surgery and choking by recognizing how these events
impacted his family members. However, despite the gravity
of the story's content, Ruland comments on survival
because of the narrative authority he exercises throughout
the piece.

Ruland first addresses the perspective of others when he
describes his mother's emotions during his heart surgery.
He writes "my mom is shocked to see mom was happy to
see it." The juxtaposition of fearful and positive emotions
creates dissonance; Ruland's mother is both afraid and
joyful. This assertion also compresses the passage of time
as he omits any signposts that would place his mother's
emotions in a clear chronology. As a result, just as the
distinction between the past and present is unclear, the

boundaries between his mother's feelings overlap.

The piece concludes with the declaration "it's happy ending." Ruland choked on a peanut, and his survival is another cause for happiness. He does not confine this sentiment of relief by using the past tense. Instead, the happy ending takes place in the present. Ruland challenges the reader to reconsider their understanding of emotions. Drawn from memories and emotions that extend beyond his own, "about my heart" suggests feelings, like people, have a capacity for survival.

The Time I Got Inspired to Build a Car of the Future

by Josh Larson

While I was in Cindy's bedroom—well actually, my bedroom at Cindy's house—I was watching an episode of *Team Umizoomi* and as soon as I saw that episode I knew I would have an everything car for me and everyone else so I focused on that and so I went and told my mom and dad about it and I wanted to make one of my own so badly but they said no and so that didn't go the way I planned and that was the day I got inspired to build a futuristic car.

My Girl
by Layne Wigfield

A pond time a boy love girl
He break her harnt
Cry girl
Runway
Home
Me love her
Kiss me
My hornt is pumping
My love
One time
2 week
past
for me. Be and
my girl love me
see me day
me. To me
be is me
me sick

girl care me
help me
me happy
sad.
Marred me
To carry
Be is cool
To me die

Hot to Handle
by Kelly McNamera

We were having free swim at the middle school pool. I was lying at the bottom of the pool on a black line under the water. They think it was because I had a seizure. A student found me underwater and screamed for the teacher. The teacher then jumped into the water, pulled me out, and gave me CPR. They called for an ambulance and I was rushed to the hospital. They say if I would have stayed underwater one more second I would have died. Everyone at school asked if I was okay. The girls all thought I was really lucky for getting mouth-to-mouth from Mr. Jackson. He was hot stuff.

Aliens in the Group Home
by Kelly Matson

This is how I would imagine an alien indicating a person in a group home. I read this book one time, *My Teacher Glows in the Dark*. It was a book about a boy who went to school in Kennituck, Connecticut. And his name was Peter. And his rival was Duncan Dugal. And what happens, there are some stories about aliens coming into their school and they disguise themselves as humans and what I thought would be funny would be something happened at a group home where, if there was a staff on their personal phone or something as playing music on their phone or just staff chatting on each other and not checking on me, then I would send an alien from Mars or Jupiter to ask the staff, "Why do you have your phone out?"

The staff would hear the robotic voice and scream. The staff would run out of the house when the other staff would hear this and would run out of the house too! The aliens would take the staff to the spacecraft. The staff would be startled. "Where are we going?" the staff would ask.

The aliens would say, "We're taking you to Jupiter and Mars."

The staff would ask, "No, you can't make us go there! Why are you taking us there?"

The aliens would say, "Because you had your cell phones on and you were playing music on it."

"No, you can't take our phones away from us!"

Spidercat
by Shelagh Winkel

Once upon a time there was a spider and a cat. The spider and the cat were walking along. A strange wind blew them into each other and they became Spidercat.

The spidercat can dance an Irish jig. It listens to Enya, eats carrots, corned beef and cabbage and loves to drink orange juice. When it loses one leg, it will grow another. Spidercats live here in Minnesota. So watch out. They like to sneak up on you and then pounce on you.

They can guard your house from burglars. They can speak Italian, and their main language is English.

Caleb's Surgery
by Caleb Gutz

When I was a baby in 1993 I had 2 holes in my heart they did the surgery in the dark with a Flash light my mom called me ugly baby then I got cuter When I was a baby I Love to eat some cake and it was on my Little Face and The cake was so Good I took a Nap thinking about my cake.

A Poetic Letter to My Great Grandpa Charlie
by Shelagh Winkel

Dear Great Grandpa Charlie,

May you feel the cool breeze against your cheeks on a cool summer day. May you feel the calmness when you are pulling out each weed from the garden. May it feel peaceful and calm and relaxing and may you become one with Nature. May those other noises—helicopters, airplanes—not distract you or disturb you. Enjoy the birds singing their songs for you. May you enjoy the Nature all around you. Be part of Nature. Feel the wind. Hear the birds singing. Feel the coolness of a cool summer day.

May your worries become like the weeds, and as you pull out each weed, may you throw out your worries along with them. All that is left is calmness. When all the weeds in your garden are gone, may all the worries in your mind be gone as well.

My Mother Is Mom
by April Robinson

Family my mother can help me can different background in the south in she in south go to church in Mississippi Abdeen Abdeen MS. She pick the cotton in the field until the sun go down in the south in Mississippi in Abdeen.

Walking Makes My Legs Stronger
by Blong Moua

I was walking to the store which is close to my house and I walked home and my legs were sore but I don't care because the more I walk then my legs get stronger.

The Authors

Mary Ayetey is a writer who has autism who writes stories about Henriette and Bobbi and Blu. She writes about everything especially fiction, poetry and songs. She makes Jewelry, Greeting Cards, Soaps and Fire Starters. She likes Game of Thrones, Wonder Woman, Star Wars, The Avengers and Stranger Things. Mary is a very nice lady and she doesn't bite.

Justin Beebe is an actor. He's played Shrek. Justin loves women's wrestling. He'd like to be in the ring with those girls, but he'd probably get his butt kicked.

Max Cookas lives in Burnsville, Minnesota. He likes making keychains, printing pictures, and eating at White Castle. His favorite color is silver and he loves the song "Slow Ride" by Foghat.

Eric Ferguson likes to play sports, play video games, and hang out with friends.

Caleb Gutz is gifted and a good friend to others. He loves going to a football game.

Stephanie Hart has a great sense of humor. She enjoys coming to Cow Tipping class and challenging herself to try new things.

Josh Larson is 24 going on 25. He came to Achieve Services in 2014. He is autistic.

Kelly Matson likes listening to Motown, the Beat Bands, or anything from the Rock 'n' Roll Era. She likes to listen to stories of the Teen School Era while going on playgrounds, walking, swimming, or doing crafts. She's looking for someone to be a dependable, trustworthy hugger. She's a warm and cozy person. She sends get well or sympathy cards to people when she knows that they need it.

Kelly McNamera is outgoing and likes going to concerts. She would like to marry Joe someday. Her family gets together on Thanksgiving and eats turkey and mashed potatoes. She likes girly things like shopping and getting her nails and hair done.

Blong Moua speaks two languages plus his background is Hmong.

Kong Moua likes reading, movies, and is a big fan of romance. He likes to draw and loves to cook in the kitchen. He likes Pepsi, and loves to swim and play board games.

April Robinson was born in Harlem, NY on 54th Street. She likes greens and cornbread. April used to roller skate and also likes to play frisbee. Football. Go walking in her free time when it's nice out. When she's bored she loves to make jewelry, draw pictures and write about all sorts of distant characters, in a fictional sense, and also loves to write about happy things. Someday April wants to open her own chiropractor business, give people massages, and have a big house where all of her friends can come and stay with her.

Danny Roherty didn't like to read and write. Harry Potter, however, changed that. He wrote he first poem and it was called "Life," an anti-suicidal poem. So then it just blossomed from there. He started his book writing and reading biographies and sci-fi or fantasy books and even wrote more poems. He thinks you all will love what he has to offer the world because he still has the imagination of a kid. One who wants to share his creativeness. To spread his imagination to the world.

Mike Ruland likes technology. It's little device. He likes sports. He watches sports. He likes movies and he likes food.

Layne Wigfield is energetic and likes to share his works. He likes sports. Layne has written many pieces about love.

Maddie Wild Crea loves reading historical fiction novels. She considers herself a fiction story writer. She began writing while in her teens. She loves Beethoven, movies and classic literature. She was interviewed on Music with Minnesotans on MPR because of her love of classical music. She lives in Saint Anthony Park, next to the University of MN with her husband, Jess. She dreams of going back to Austria at some time in her life, to pay her respects to her two favorite classical composers, Beethoven and Mozart.

Shelagh Winkel has been writing since she was in grade school. She loves dancing, singing and writing. She has created and written about many magical creatures and she has an extensive and ever-expanding unicorn collection.